THIS LAND CALLED AMERICA: **HAWAII**

CREATIVE EDUCATION

Published by Creative Education
P.O. Box 227, Mankato, Minnesota 56002
Creative Education is an imprint of The Creative Company
www.thecreativecompany.us

Book and cover design by Blue Design (www.bluedes.com)
Art direction by Rita Marshall
Printed in the United States of America

Photographs by Alamy (David Fleetham), Corbis (James L. Amos,
Bettmann, Richard A. Cooke, Thomas Frey, NASA, Michael T. Sedam,
Jim Sugar, Swim Ink 2 LLC), Getty Images (Altrendo Travel, Ira Block,
Ann Cecil, Eliot Elisofon//Time Life Pictures, Jules Frazier Photography,
Jonathan Kingston, David Muench, Panoramic Images, Lew Robertson,
Stock Montage/Stock Montage, Time & Life Pictures, Chris van
Lennep)

Library of Congress Cataloging-in-Publication Data
Shofner, Shawndra.
Hawaii / by Shawndra Shofner.
p. cm. — (This land called America)
Includes bibliographical references and index.
ISBN 978-1-58341-636-5
1. Hawaii—Juvenile literature. I. Title. II. Series.
DU623.25.S56 2008
996.9—dc22   2007005706

First Edition
9 8 7 6 5 4 3 2 1

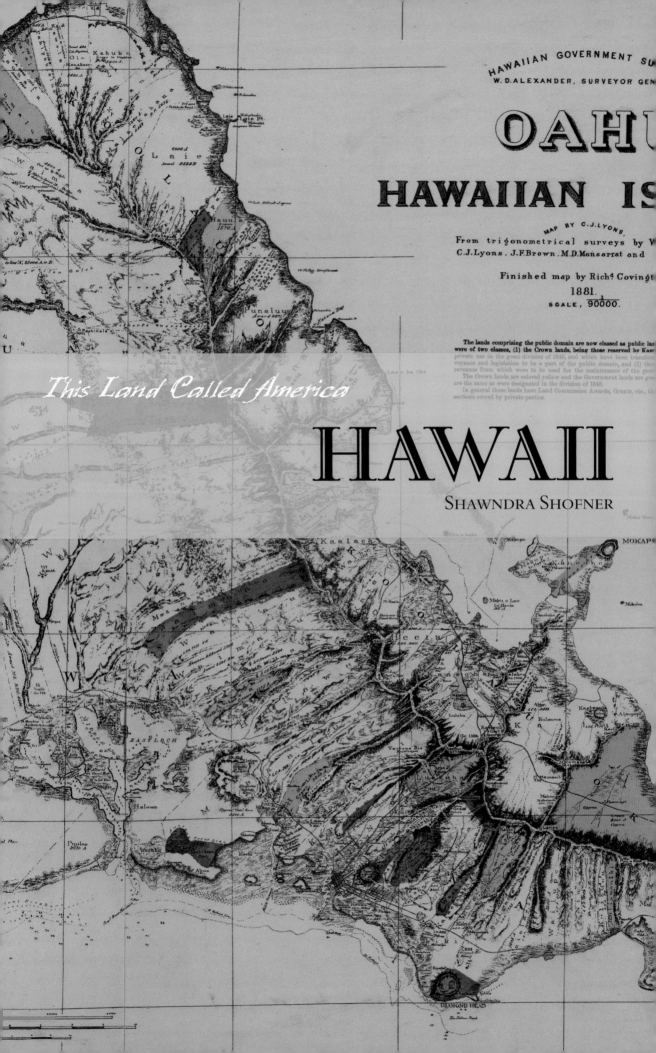

This Land Called America

HAWAII

Shawndra Shofner

THIS LAND CALLED AMERICA

Hawaii

SHAWNDRA SHOFNER

STEEP WAVES CURL, THEN CRASH AGAINST OAHU'S
NORTH SHORE. ALL DAY LONG, TANNED SURFERS
IN COLORFUL SWIMSUITS CARRY LONG, SKINNY
BOARDS INTO THE OCEAN. LYING ON THE BOARDS,
THEY PADDLE OUT AND WAIT IN LINE TO CATCH
A WAVE. SOME STAND UP TOO SOON, WOBBLE,
AND WIPE OUT. OTHERS, KNEES BENT AND BACKS
STRAIGHT, CARVE BACK AND FORTH ACROSS
THE WAVE'S WALL, RIDING IT TO THE END. ONE
DAREDEVIL CATCHES SOME AIR. ANOTHER SPINS
A FULL CIRCLE WITHOUT FALLING. JUST AS IT DID
WHEN THE FIRST HAWAIIANS INVENTED SURFING,
THE TROPICAL PLAYGROUND OF HAWAII THRILLS
PEOPLE EVERY DAY.

From Kingdom to State

THE HAWAIIAN ISLANDS' FIRST SETTLERS CAME FROM THE MARQUESAS ISLANDS IN THE SOUTH PACIFIC OCEAN ALMOST 2,000 YEARS AGO. THESE PEOPLE ROWED LARGE CANOES ACROSS THE VAST OCEAN. THEY USED THE STARS, OCEAN CURRENTS, AND FLIGHT PATTERNS OF BIRDS TO GUIDE THEIR WAY. THE FIRST HAWAIIANS DID NOT HAVE A WRITTEN LANGUAGE.

A Native of Otaheite defying his Enemy by the Wry Mouth.

A New Zealand Warrior defying his Enemies.

A Musical Youth in the Habit of his Profession.

An Ape of Java.

Habits of a Woman & Boy.

Habit of a Priest.

The Hooded Serpent.

They passed on their history by singing chants and telling stories. People today know what the first Hawaiians' lives were like because they carved pictures into rocks. Some of these pictures, called petroglyphs, show that they knew how to surf. They drew stick people riding long boards on the water.

Around A.D. 1100, others came to Hawaii from the Society Islands southwest of the Marquesas Islands. People settled on Hawaii's seven largest islands, and each island was ruled by a different king. Some people raised chickens and pigs. Others grew bananas and sugar cane. Still others built huge temples in which the king worshipped the gods of the universe. Many

The natives of Hawaii and other nearby islands (above) may not have had a written language, but they communicated by pictures (opposite).

YEAR

1810 King Kamehameha I unifies seven islands, creating the Kingdom of Hawaii.

EVENT

served in the king's army. Wars between the island kingdoms were common. In 1810, King Kamehameha I united the main islands. He ruled them as the Kingdom of Hawaii.

The first European to visit Hawaii was English captain James Cook. He named the new land "The Sandwich Islands," after the Earl of Sandwich, the man who had funded Cook's journey. Hawaiians on the islands of Kauai and Niihau welcomed Captain Cook and his crew in awe on January 20, 1778. They thought he was a god and treated him with great respect. But when one of his crew members died on another visit the next year, the Hawaiians understood that Cook was not a god. The people became angry because they had given the "gods" large quantities of supplies. One day, a chief stole one of Cook's boats. Cook tried to kidnap another chief and trade him for the boat. The angry Hawaiians defended their chief. They killed Cook on the beach of Kealakekua Bay. The rest of Cook's men barely escaped.

Trading ships on routes to and from Asia used Cook's maps to find Hawaii. Captains docked their ships on the islands to replenish food and water supplies. Books about this beautiful place led to visits by explorers, tourists, and fishermen. Some

Before Kamehameha I came to power, famed explorer James Cook made several trips to the Pacific islands.

Kamehameha I was a good businessman who knew how to make his kingdom rich and successful.

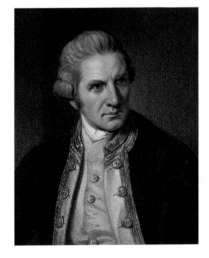

YEAR

1835   Farming begins on Kauai's first sugar cane plantation.

EVENT

- 9 -

Queen Liliuokalani was the first and only Hawaiian queen, taking the throne after her two brothers died.

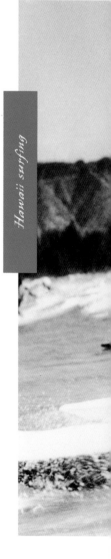

travelers eventually made the islands their home. Missionaries came to Hawaii in 1820 and shared their Christian beliefs. They taught the Hawaiians how to read and write. They also introduced new medicines to the native people.

Soon, European and American settlers started large sugar cane and pineapple farms in Hawaii. These plantations took over much of the land. When Hawaiian Queen Liliuokalani rose to power in 1891, she tried to decrease the control that regular citizens, such as plantation owners, had. But, two years later, the powerful plantation owners removed her from power. They ruled themselves as the Republic of Hawaii for five years. In 1900, the United States claimed Hawaii as a territory.

Hawaii was admitted as the 50th and final U.S. state on August 21, 1959. Church bells rang in Honolulu when U.S. President Dwight Eisenhower signed the official proclamation. The first U.S. flag with 50 stars for 50 states was raised on July 4, 1960, at Fort McHenry National Monument in Maryland.

YEAR

1853   A smallpox epidemic kills 5,000 native Hawaiians.

EVENT

Surfing and canoeing
have been popular
oceanside activities in
Hawaii for hundreds
of years.

Pacific Island Paradise

HAWAII IS THE ONLY U.S. STATE THAT IS NOT ON THE CONTINENT OF NORTH AMERICA. HAWAII'S 132 ISLANDS ARE LOCATED IN THE MIDDLE OF THE NORTH PACIFIC OCEAN NEAR THE TROPIC OF CANCER. VOLCANOES FORMED ALL OF THE MAJOR ISLANDS AROUND SIX MILLION YEARS AGO. HAWAII IS SITUATED ABOUT AS FAR SOUTH AS CENTRAL MEXICO. IT IS THE SOUTHERNMOST STATE.

Sea turtles, humpback whales, and porpoises make their home in the ocean waters around Hawaii. Birds such as the honeycreeper and coot also live on the islands. The monk seal and hoary bat are the only mammals native to Hawaii. The first settlers brought pigs, horses, sheep, and goats, and many of those animals roam wild on the islands today.

People live on seven of the state's islands. The largest island, Hawaii, is the southernmost. Arcing northwest from Hawaii are the islands of Maui, Lanai, Molokai, Oahu, Kauai, and Niihau.

People call Hawaii "Big Island" to avoid confusing it with the state of Hawaii. Big Island has two active volcanoes. Mauna Loa and Kilauea erupt every few years, sending streams of red-hot lava trickling into the ocean. On Big Island's western coast, the beaches shimmer with black sand from the crushed lava.

Adult green sea turtles eat algae found near Hawaii's shorelines and coral reefs.

One of the largest inactive volcanoes in the world is eastern Maui's Haleakala. It last erupted around 1790, adding new land to the island. Maui farmers grow sugar cane, pineapple, onions, and flowers, such as bird of paradise and pink ginger. Hawaii's state bird, the nene (a type of goose), and the rare silversword plant also thrive on Maui.

Sugar cane is grown today on about 70,000 acres (28,328 ha) on the islands of Maui (pictured) and Kauai.

YEAR

1863 Kauai resident Elizabeth Sinclair purchases Niihau Island for $10,000.

EVENT

- 13 -

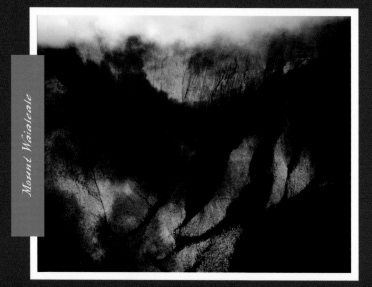

In 1922, businessman James Dole purchased the island of Lanai for $1.1 million. He planted pineapples in the island's rich fields. He then canned the sweet, juicy fruit and began shipping it around the world.

The northern coast of Molokai is home to the world's tallest sea cliffs. Papohaku Beach on Molokai's west coast boasts a three-mile (4.8 km) white sand beach. Farmers grow macadamia nuts and coffee beans on the island's central plain.

Oahu's Waikiki beach attracts thousands of tourists every year. Visitors to the island often tour Diamond Head crater on the southeastern end of Oahu. A volcanic explosion that

Hawaii's landscape is full of unique and spectacular geological features such as Kauai's Mount Waialeale (above) and Molokai's sea cliffs (opposite), which are 2,000 feet (610 m) tall.

1874   The "Merry Monarch," David Kalakaua, ascends the Hawaiian throne.

Oahu's Waikiki beach has to import its white sand because the ocean constantly erodes the beachfront.

occurred about 500,000 years ago left behind the crater, which is more than 3,500 feet (1,067 m) in diameter.

Mount Waialeale on the island of Kauai is the rainiest spot on Earth. More than 460 inches (1,168 cm) of rain fall on the mountain each year. Waters that flowed from Mount Waialeale carved the Waimea Canyon. Nicknamed the "Grand Canyon of the Pacific," it is 10 miles (16 km) long, 2 miles (3.2 km) wide, and more than 3,500 feet (1,067 m) deep.

The smallest of Hawaii's settled islands, Niihau, lies 17 miles (27 km) off the west coast of Kauai. Kauai resident Elizabeth Sinclair, who made a fortune from selling land that she owned in New Zealand, bought Niihau in 1863 for $10,000. Her descendants still own much of the island. Jewelers today use rare Niihau shells to make expensive necklaces.

Hawaiians enjoy warm weather year-round. There are only two seasons: summer, from May to October, and winter, from November to April. The average daytime temperature is 85 °F (29 °C) in the summer and 78 °F (26 °C) in the winter.

Only the tops of the volcanoes that made the Hawaiian Islands can be seen from space.

YEAR
1900 Hawaii becomes a U.S. territory and is governed by Hawaiian Sanford Dole.
EVENT

- *17* -

A Welcoming Land

MANY VISITORS FIRST CAME TO HAWAII IN THE 1800S AFTER READING ABOUT THE ISLANDS' NATURAL BEAUTY. UNFORTUNATELY, THE VISITORS BROUGHT DISEASES SUCH AS INFLUENZA, MEASLES, AND WHOOPING COUGH WITH THEM. MANY NATIVE PEOPLE DIED. PLANTATION OWNERS WERE LEFT WITHOUT ENOUGH PEOPLE TO WORK IN THE FIELDS. SO THE OWNERS BROUGHT IN

workers from other countries. Thousands came from China, Japan, and the Philippines in the late 1800s. More people arrived from Korea, Puerto Rico, Portugal, and Samoa in the early 1900s.

Today, those people's descendants make up most of Hawaii's population. Many others move to Hawaii every year to work or retire. Hawaii's citizens enjoy different cultures, ocean sports, beautiful views, and warm weather year-round.

About two-thirds of Hawaii's population is Asian American. These are people with Chinese, Japanese, Filipino, or Korean roots. The first Chinese-American U.S. senator was

For generations, native Hawaiian women, dressed in traditional costumes, have entertained crowds with their hula dancing (above and opposite).

Larger surfboards help people ride big waves, while smaller boards help them ride small waves.

Hiram L. Fong from Oahu. He held office from 1959 to 1977. George Ariyoshi from Big Island was elected in 1974 as Hawaii's first Japanese-American governor.

White people make up about 30 percent of Hawaii's population. The remaining 10 percent consists of Hispanic Americans, African Americans, and partially native Hawaiians. Only about 9,000 people are fully native Hawaiian today.

Tourism is Hawaii's top industry. More than seven million visitors come from around the globe to vacation on the islands each year. Many Hawaiians have jobs in resorts, restaurants, golf courses, and entertainment.

Native Hawaiian customs are especially popular among tourists in Hawaii. Early Hawaiians made leis, or necklaces,

YEAR
1901 James Dole's canned pineapple enables people far from Hawaii to enjoy the tropical fruit.
EVENT

Franklin Delano Roosevelt becomes the first U.S. president to visit Hawaii.

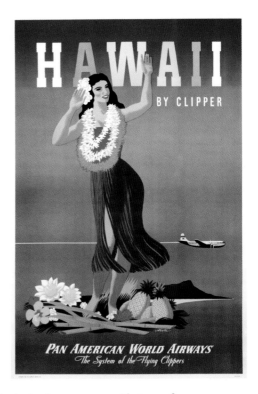

The image of a Hawaiian woman hula dancing has long been used to advertise the islands to tourists.

Hawaiian coastline

from seashells, flowers, or feathers. These were given to another person as a token of affection. Today, visitors to Hawaii are welcomed with flower leis. The hula is a traditional Hawaiian dance that tells a story. The first Hawaiians used the hula as a form of prayer. Now hula lessons and flashy hula shows are more common. Resorts regularly put on luaus for their guests. Luaus are large parties with food, music, and hula dancing.

Surfing is a native Hawaiian sport used by Hawaii's first kings to display their courage and power. Their surfboards were very heavy. They were made from the wood of the Hawaiian koa tree. Surfers today use boards made from lighter materials such as plastic and fiberglass. Learning how to surf is a popular activity for tourists.

People from around the world quickly recognize the melody and refrain to "Aloha Oe," one of the most famous Hawaiian songs. It was written by Queen Liliuokalani in 1878. She was the last queen to rule the islands. Many well-known singers, including Elvis Presley, made recordings of this beautiful goodbye song.

YEAR
1935
EVENT
Amelia Earhart is the first pilot to fly solo from Honolulu to Oakland, California.

Singer Don Ho

Hawaiian singer Don Ho performed live concerts five evenings a week at a resort in Waikiki until his death in 2007. He is best known for his hit song "Tiny Bubbles." From 1976 to 1977, he hosted *The Don Ho Show* on network television.

In addition to tourism and entertainment, farming is a major industry in Hawaii. Pineapple, sugar cane, and nursery plants are the state's chief products. Farmers also grow coffee beans, bananas, and macadamia nuts. Ranchers raise cattle and sheep. Food processing and clothing are other main industries.

Singer Don Ho (above, with actress Barbara Eden in 1968) grew up on the island of Oahu, where Dole pineapples (opposite) are grown today in abundance.

Everything Exotic

FEASTS FOR THE EYES APPEAR ON EVERY HAWAIIAN ISLAND. THE ROYAL IOLANI PALACE ON OAHU, WHERE KINGS AND QUEENS LIVED UNTIL 1893, IS A GRAND EXAMPLE. ANOTHER FAMOUS BUILDING IS THE HULIHE'E PALACE. LOCATED ON BIG ISLAND, IT WAS BUILT FROM MATERIALS NATIVE TO HAWAII SUCH AS LAVA ROCK AND KOA TIMBER. AFTER GOVERNOR JOHN ADAMS KUAKINI

lived there from 1838 to 1844, Hawaiian royalty often used it as a vacation home. In October 2006, two earthquakes caused more than $1 million in damage to the Hulihe'e Palace. As of 2007, efforts were underway to repair the historic building.

The Spouting Horn on Kauai is a strange sight to see. Ocean waves roll under a lava shelf, where water pressure steadily builds. A small hole in the shelf allows some water to escape. The spray then shoots—or spouts—almost 50 feet (15 m) into the air. A rainbow shimmers through the spray when the sun hits the mist.

The rock gardens on Lanai are unlike any other natural place on the planet. The area is named Keahikawelo, or Garden of the Gods. It looks like the surface of the moon. Big and small boulders dot the dry land. The stones turn shades of red and purple with the morning or evening sun.

YEAR
1946 A great tsunami wave kills more than 150 people in Big Island's city of Hilo.
EVENT

Hawaii provides the perfect backdrop for sporting events such as the Ironman triathlon.

Oahu's Pearl Harbor is home to the USS *Arizona* Memorial. The building was constructed over a battleship that was sunk when Japan attacked the U.S. ships on December 7, 1941. The memorial honors the 1,177 crew members who lost their lives aboard the *Arizona*.

There are no professional sports teams in Hawaii. But Hawaii's Aloha Stadium in Honolulu hosts many events. The best college football players in the U.S. face off in the annual Hawaii Bowl and Hula Bowl at the stadium. National Football League players compete there in the Pro Bowl that is held one week after the Super Bowl. Soccer matches and baseball games are played in Aloha Stadium, too.

YEAR

1979 Hawaiian Airlines operates the first scheduled flight to have an all-female flight crew.

EVENT

Hawaiians have many legends to explain the existence of the rare Garden of the Gods rock formations.

Honolulu

Each October, 1,700 athletes compete in the Ford Ironman World Championship, a triathlon, or three-event race, held on Big Island. Participants first swim 2.4 miles (3.9 km) in the ocean. Then they race on bicycles for 112 miles (180 km). Finally, they run a 26.2-mile (42.2 km) marathon.

Big Island's Merry Monarch Hula Festival began more than 40 years ago. The April festival is named after King David Kalakaua, who loved music and dance. Hawaiians attend a week of activities, such as arts-and-crafts fairs, a parade, and hula shows. Hula dance contests between groups and single dancers are the highlight of the festival.

The entire state of Hawaii puts on two months' worth of celebrations in the fall. The Aloha Festivals have been a state tradition for 60 years. The festivals honor Hawaii's history and people. More than 300 events take place on 6 islands. There are concerts, hula contests, parades, and fishing competitions. The Aloha Festivals end in October.

Hawaiians often join together in celebrations and traditions that honor their unique culture. They also work to protect their state's natural wonders and historical places. Because of Hawaiians' dedication, visitors and residents alike will be able to celebrate for years to come the culture and splendor of these islands, some of the world's most beautiful places.

YEAR
2006   A major earthquake shakes Big Island in October, causing blackouts and landslides.
EVENT

QUICK FACTS

Population: 1,285,498

Largest city: Honolulu (pop. 380,149)

Capital: Honolulu

Entered the union: August 21, 1959

Nickname: Aloha State

State flower: hibiscus

State bird: Hawaiian goose (nene)

Size: 10,931 sq mi (28,311 sq km)—43rd-biggest in U.S.

Major industries: tourism, agriculture, food processing

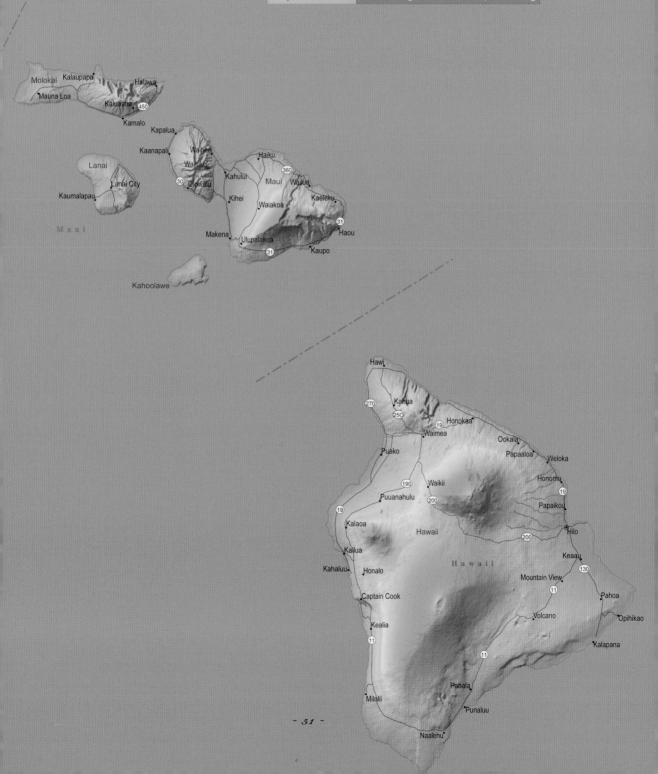

BIBLIOGRAPHY

Aloha-Hawaii. "Natural Hawaii." Tsunami Marketing. http://www.aloha-hawaii.com.

Bockenhauer, Mark H., and Stephen F. Cunha. *National Geographic: Our Fifty States.* Washington: National Geographic, 2004.

Hintz, Martin. *Hawai'i.* New York: Children's Press, 1999.

Kummer, Patricia. *Hawaii.* Mankato, Minn.: Bridgestone Books, 1997.

SHG Resources. "Hawaii Firsts, Facts, and Trivia." State Handbook and Guide Resources. http://www.shgresources .com/hi/facts.

Thompson, David, et al. *Pauline Frommer's Hawaii.* Hoboken, N.J.: Wiley Publishing, 2006.

INDEX